AF266736

ABOVE THE RUSHES

Sheila Smith McKoy

Above the Rushes

©2026 Sheila Smith McKoy
All Rights Reserved

First Printing

ISBN 978-1-970860-98-6

Cover Photo Credit: Morgan Crutchfield, 2025

ADVANCE PRAISE

Sheila Smith McKoy's *Above the Rushes* is rich in images that present her perception of nature and human nature, as exemplified in these two beautiful haiku ("scattered leaves / warmth / of the Indian Ocean" and "last night of winter— / I trace your lips with my fingers / stained glass window"), which stimulate one sense for another to enrich a physical experience and an aesthetic appreciation of life to balance an inner and outer self.

John Zhen, author of *Dreaminations* and editor of *Conversations with Lenard D. Moore*

While Sheila Smith McKoy's offering of haiku is at times dreamlike, a mysterious rush of nightmares, readers can also bask in the wonders and fertile grounds of Africa. With attention to its rich earth of flora, wildlife, and ruins, her exploration haiku is infused with texture and harmony. It is evident that Smith McKoy revels in the discovery of ancestral roots and connections, yet, she also accomplishes haiku that grounds us in those present, ephemeral moments:

dead deer lies
near the curve
off-white lily

In this first collection of haiku, we are offered and can indulge in the wide breadth of her closely sketched life journeys.

Crystal Simone Smith, author of *Ebbing Shore* and *Runagate: Songs of the Freedom Bound*

Haiku writing is a journey; this book captures Sheila's. The haiku are about nature, family, arts, music and urban life. The book opens with a breath of fresh sea wind, captured beautifully in the 'scattered leaves' haiku. The author is bold and creative in the arrangement of pieces, we see a mixture: haiku followed by a haiku sequence, a meaningful bridge that takes the reader, from 'below the rushes' to *Above the Rushes* – a place the author wants us to arrive!

Some of my favorite haiku include, 'ornate carved door': an African haiku with an African season word, 'misty sunset' and 'above the rushes'. This is one haiku book to have, a beautiful blend of nature-filled and urban haiku!
     Emmanuel Kalusian, Co-founding Editor of *The Mamba* and
                                    Africa Haiku Network.

The haiku and haiku sequences in this collection bring together the worlds of nature, personal relationships, and dreams through lush imagery and innovative juxtapositions. Smith McKoy engages our senses and reveals surprising connections between the ordinary and the sublime, offering insights that deepen with each reading.
     Ce Rosenow, senior editor of *Juxtapositions: Research and Scholarship in Haiku* and editor of *Beyond Haiku: Japanese Forms in American Poetry*

Sheila Smith McKoy's book *Above The Rushes* is a tour de force; her haiku and sequences about Africa are memorable as they unravel with vivid imagery and good details. For example, her poem "sunset sky/leopard asleep in a tree/wild berries" contrasts such vastness with small beauty in the natural world. Her poems evoke emotions, brush colors on the canvas of the reader's mind, and inspires one to pick up pen to write haiku.

Above The Rushes is the book to teach about the African landscape; it also strums one's heart strings with the rhythms of jazz. Please read this book, because this writer highly recommends it for its American and African American historical contribution to the genre of poetry, particularly haiku. Let your sensory perceptions experience this feat.
     Lenard D. Moore, author of *The Geography of Jazz*

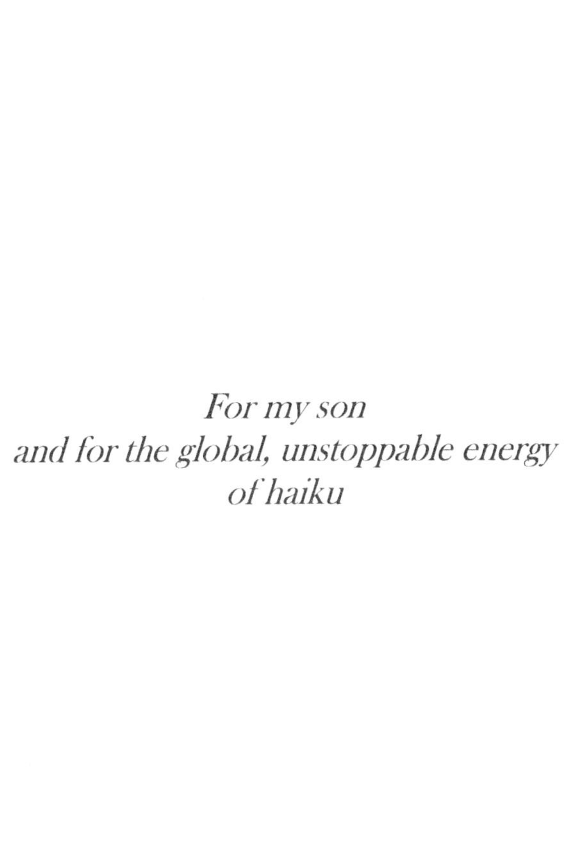

*For my son
and for the global, unstoppable energy
of haiku*

ABOVE THE RUSHES

scattered leaves
warmth
of the Indian Ocean

fire ants
trail the dry path
wild green morenga

bushbuck stands
on dry, rocky mound
crushed red grapes

just at daybreak
lions roar
steamy-hot tea

sunset sky
leopard asleep in a tree
wild redberries

banks of the Nile
wild water rushing
cracked bird egg

source of the Nile
bubbles up in the lake
bright copper pennies

Crumpled Paper

crumpled paper
on the writer's floor
winter avocados

    old newspaper
    summer storm
    erases the path

        yellowed letter
        snap beans vines
        entwine corn stalks

            glittery greeting card
            pastel flag
            blows in the breeze

chilly spring morning
lone buffalo grazes
night terrors

dust surrounds
migrating zebra herd
white-hot coals

rainbow above
mountain waterfall
braided money tree

sun breaks clouds over
bent-backed rice farmers
papyrus flowers

starlit summery night—
scented by cherry blossoms
silent obituary reading

frog mating calls
at onset of evening
weaverbird's nest

dry corn stalks
chefs cook on the beach
by the sugarcane juicer

Dreams

he haunts my dreams
belying his death
summer sunset hike

amethyst by my bed
to invite sweet dreams
broken photo frame

one red feather
on the porch
forgotten dream

startled from nightmares
lone deer
under my crab apple tree

tropical night
bent green banana fronds
mirror shards

ornate carved door
inside the locked gate
roasted cocoyam

birds of paradise soar
at nightfall
white cat napping

on the veld
antelopes startle and run
torn tarot card

dandelion spores
we startle a serval cat
as afternoon breaks

terror attack
muted news anchor
red riverbed

trumpet blares
near Table Mountain
black-and-white photo

Secrets

January-blooming
crepe myrtle tree
snow forecast

we have not told her
she lives here now
mossy river rock

I envy that hawk
flying high, free
small fall garden

misty sunset
miserable ways
to make a living

wild dogs' barks
echo across the meadow
haunted dreams

moose antlers rise
above the rushes
too-tiny caskets

public square statues
covered by pigeon droppings
sea urchin shell

savannah grass
swaying in the wind
lost phone charger

dead deer lies
near the curve
off-white lily

tadpoles swim
in mid-Spring
crushed beer can

last night of winter—
I trace your lips with my fingers
stained glass window

The Other Side of the Fence

white picket fence
bean vines wrap
around corn stalks

   broken glass
   near a barbed wire fence
   snowy baby's breath

      Kilimanjaro sun
      roses vine
      around the split rails

         ancient iron fence
         wrought unknown hands
         East Bay fog

torn manuscript
ancient tree limbs
touch the ground

web-sitting spider
awaits prey at sunset
homemade wine

open water snorkeling
a tiger shark beneath me
antique cracked mirror

kudzu weight down
the old gate
tethered blue kite

Mayflowers bloom
on my birthday
bobwhite calls

russet and yellow sunset
at summer's end
carved wooden masks

Taking Time

opportunities
now lost
jazz drummer

river-rusted boat
at long last
we start anew

coyote runs
in front of my car
African time

late autumn sunset
she looks for love
in his eyes

shadows
of prison bars
cresting rapids

homeless encampment
crowd city limit sign
shafts of moonlight

mossy cliff
on the mountain trail
crested moon

train whistle
warbling tree swallow
high in the tree

grey-blue heron
tromps the lakeshore
pickleball court

wind-blown
maypole ribbons
mud dauber nest

photos decorate the
Dia de los Muertos altar
scattered hyacinths

ABOUT THE AUTHOR

Sheila Smith McKoy, PHD is an award-winning poet, fiction writer, autoethnographer, and filmmaker. The recipient of the 2020 Muriel Craft Bailey Memorial Prize in poetry, her full-length poetry collection, *The Bones Beneath* (Black Lawrence Press, 2024) is "a haunting work that transcends temporal boundaries." She is also co-author of *One Window's Light: A Haiku Collection*, the 2017 Haiku Society of America's Merit Book Award for best haiku anthology and *Griots: Keepers of the Story*, a haibun collection (2026), both of which were written in collaboration with four Black poets. Her fiction has appeared in *FIYAH*, *Infinite Worlds* and *Obsidian* among others. Smith McKoy has also written, produced, directed or served as executive producer for four documentary films, including *Maama Watali* and *Luwero: A Conversation about War, Peace and Gender* (2017). In addition to her poetry and fiction, Smith McKoy has authored and edited numerous scholarly works. She is published widely as a scholar and activist focused on race and difference, mentorship, literature and culture. A native of Raleigh, NC, returned to her hometown in 2024.

www.ingramcontent.com/pod-product-compliance
Lightning Source LLC
Chambersburg PA
CBHW050017040726
47599CB00014B/1424